Strength Training for V

A special thank you to: Fiona Warneke, Alicia King, Guy Leech and Mark Donaldson, Photography

The Body Coach Series

Strength Training for Women

Build Stronger Bones,
Leaner Muscles and a Firmer Body
with Australia's Body Coach®

Paul Collins

Meyer & Meyer Sport

British Library Cataloguing in Publication Data
A catalogue record for this book is available from the British Library

Paul Collins
Strength Training for Women
Maidenhead: Meyer & Meyer Sport (UK) Ltd., 2009
ISBN 978-1-84126-248-2

© 2009 by Paul Collins (text & photos)
and Meyer & Meyer Sport (UK) Ltd. (Layout)
Aachen, Adelaide, Auckland, Budapest, Cape Town, Graz, Indianapolis,
Maidenhead, New York, Olten (CH), Singapore, Toronto
Member of the World
Sport Publishers' Association (WSPA)
www.w-s-p-a.org
Printed and bound by: B.O.S.S Druck und Medien GmbH, Germany
ISBN 978-1-84126-248-2
E-Mail: verlag@m-m-sports.com
www.m-m-sports.com

Contents

Introduction

Welcome!

I'm The Body Coach®, Paul Collins, your exclusive personal coach here to guide and motivate you towards a stronger and leaner body. The combination of strength training, aerobic exercise and healthy eating habits have shown to be the most effective for fat loss and muscle toning. Muscle toning through strength training is simply the simultaneous decrease of body fat and restoration of lean muscle tissue. While aerobic exercise burns fat during exercise, anaerobic exercises, like strength training, utilize fat hours after exercise. Strength training can also increase the metabolic rate by restoring muscle tissue that had been lost over the years from a sedentary lifestyle and reduce the risk of osteoporosis by building stronger bones.

It's a fact that every year after the age of 30, the average person gains one pound of body weight yet loses up to half a pound of muscle. Consequently, our resting metabolism decreases approximately 0.05 percent every year. Furthermore, one pound of muscle burns approximately 30-50 calories (125-210 kilojoules) per day. In contrast, a pound of fat only burns about three calories (12 kilojoules) per day. This may not seem significant considering one pound of fat contains approximately 3500 calories (14,700 kilojoules), but over the course of years, it all adds up. Proper aerobic and strength exercise and healthy eating habits can help reverse this process.

Strength Training for Women has been developed as a training guide as more women understand the health benefits of strength training and more women-only fitness centers continue to pop up around the world. In light of this, the myths of women gaining large muscles have also been dispelled as the potential for muscle growth (hypertrophy) is not as great as men due mainly to the lower levels of testosterone in women. What will happen with strength training though is the way the body changes shape as fat is reduced and lean muscle tissue maintained.

Paul Collins with World Ironman champion Guy Leech

Strength Training for Women is written in five parts. **First,** I will educate you about general strength training terminology. **Second**, I will help you pinpoint the major muscle groups of the body and provide Strength Training exercises used in a gym using hand weights (dumbbells), barbells, various cable, pin-loaded and weighted machines. **Third**, I will provide you with a series of strength training routines for use in the gym. **Fourth**, is a body weight workout routine that can be performed at home or whilst travelling. **Fifth,** is the take anywhere hand weight routine for the whole body.

Through regular participation in strength training, many women find a positive outcome with body image, confidence and self-esteem. This is because each strength training session requires a certain amount of self-discipline and concentration which brings with it a feeling of accomplishment. Always check with your doctor before beginning exercise if you have any medical conditions or are pregnant.

I look forward to working with you!

Paul Collins
The Body Coach®

www.thebodycoach.com

About the Author

Paul Collins has made his career teaching people how to get fit, lose weight, look good and feel great. Coaching since age 14, Paul has personally trained world-class athletes and teams in a variety of sports including members of the Australian Olympic Swimming Team.

Paul was an outstanding athlete in his own right having played grade rugby league in the national competition. He is also an A-grade squash player, Australian Budokan Karate champion and NSW Masters Athletes State Track and Field Champion.

Combining an athletic and sports background with a Bachelor of Physical Education degree and national certification as a Strength and Conditioning Coach and Personal Trainer, Paul is a key presenter to the Australian Track and Field Coaching Association, Australia Swimming Coaches and Teachers Association, NSW Squash Academy, Australian Karate Team, Australian Rugby League and the Australian Fitness Industry and travels internationally to present a highly entertaining series of corporate Health and Well-being Seminars and exclusive Five-star Personal Training.

Paul is General Manager of the Australian Academy of Sport and Fitness (AASF) in Sydney, Australia – a fitness college for international (overseas) students with 3-month to 2-year visa courses towards becoming a gym instructor personal trainer - visit: www.sportandfitness.com.au

For more details go to: www.thebodycoach.com

Chapter 1

Building Stronger Bones

Welcome to Strength Training for Women – the essential guide for building stronger bones, leaner muscles and a firmer body. As your personal Body Coach® my role is to guide and motivate you through a series of strength training exercises that will help tone and reshape your whole body. With adequate muscular strength and endurance you will find daily activities become easier with less fatigue. Your balance will improve as well as your muscular coordination and posture.

Strength training for women has many benefits:

- Strengthening bones and protection against osteoporosis
- Toning, firming and reshaping muscles
- Improving overall body shape and posture
- Improving muscular strength and endurance
- Enhancing heart and lung function
- Helping control blood pressure
- Improving nervous system function
- Maintaining a healthy body weight

The focus of this book is based upon guiding you through the basic strength exercises most commonly available in a gym. The aim is to provide you with the essential knowledge and understanding of putting these into practice and help build your confidence to progress further in your training endeavours. By providing you with the basic fundamentals of strength training you will be able to link the theory and practical aspects together through regular practice contributing to a positive self-image and understanding of a proper and most effective work out routine.

Overcoming the Fears

The strength training area was once upon a time dominated by men. But with the introduction of women only fitness centers over the past decade, women are now starting to reap the benefits of having their own training facility. As more and more women venture into the gym to lift weights, many of the myths once held are being broken.

One of the main myths associated with strength training for women is the concern of building larger muscles. Instead, what most women are finding is the exact opposite – in that strength training helps tone, firm and reshape the body. You see, it's a myth that strength training makes women bulk up. The major difference is due the amount of testosterone produced by the body in men and women. Since women have only a fraction of the testosterone men have, there's no need to worry about bulking up.

Quite often, the feeling of a 'muscle burning' or being 'pumped up' after completing a set of repetitions, lifting heavy weights, can often be misinterpreted as bulking-up, when in fact it is a short term response of the blood pooling in this area to supply more oxygen and taking away unwanted carbon dioxide and lactic acid build-up. After a short period of time for removal and repair, this feeling will subside. But because it maybe a new feeling to most women, it can often be mistaken as bulking-up. As lean muscle is more compact than fat, over time strength training will actually strip muscle size making you smaller, rather than larger and look more toned.

The other known effect that may cause a feeling of bulkiness is what is known as the DOMS effect (Delayed Onset Muscle Soreness). Approximately 24-48 hours after lifting weights for the first time, changing a program or training too hard the body will often respond with a period of muscular tension and soreness whilst the body and muscles repair themselves. In saying this, it is important to start off any training using light weights only in a supervised environment for the first few weeks until the body, its muscles, tendons and joints adapt. The DOMS effect is often associated with any new activity the body undergoes from horseback riding to running and waterskiing, especially after a long lay-off. This is why a proper warm-up before exercising and a cooldown and gentle stretch after exercising are so vital in reducing muscular soreness and recovery. Although it may be rewarding for some people to feel sore after their workouts, if they ease back into training they will be able to resume subsequent workouts sooner with greater intensity and with less chance of injury.

Starting Point

Sets and **repetitions** are the building blocks of your strength training routine. A repetition (or rep) is one complete execution of an exercise. So, for example, one rep of a squat exercise would be the full cycle squatting down and then back up. In scientific terms, this is called an eccentric (negative or down part) and concentric (positive or up part) of the squat movement. I mention these terms because over time you will hear a number of new words used to describe an exercise or movement that mean exactly the same thing, but in a more complex scientific way. In our case, we'll keep it simple. Each repetition should also move through its full range of motion. In the case of the bench press exercise, this means pushing the weight up (concentric) until your arms are straight, then lowering it back down (eccentric) towards the chest without stopping. The specific number of sets and repetitions are determined by ones training objective. Strength training itself is built upon a general training cycle as follows:

Strength Training Cycles

	Beginner or restarting	General Conditioning	Strength	Power	Maintenance
Sets	1-3	1-3	2-5	2-5	1-2
Reps	10-15	10-12	6-8	3-5	6-10
Percentage (%) of maximium	40-50%	50-60%	60-80%	65-90%	50-80%
Intensity	low	moderate	high	high	moderate
Volume	moderate	moderate/high	moderate	low	moderate

A training cycle is generally applied over a 4-week period. For instance, the general conditioning cycle maybe performed over 4 weeks, before moving on to strength cycle for 4 weeks and so forth. As strength and muscle coordination improves during this 4-week period a small increase in the weight being lifted can be applied or a new exercise for the same muscle group introduced.

THE BODY COACH

In the chart above you will notice a percentage (%) of maximum range. This refers to the maximum number of repetitions that can be achieved lifting a specific weight. For example, 60-80% refers to performing 6-8 repetitions of an exercise at which a point of muscle fatigue sets in. In advanced training, these percentiles are calculated by performing a one repetition maximum lift. But when first starting out, there is a period of 8-12 weeks where the body needs to adapt appropriately before these tests are undertaken – under the supervision of a qualified fitness professional. In the beginning, using a light weight that fulfills the required amount of reps will give you the starting point to build from as your knowledge and understanding increases. As the body adapts quickly and needs new variables, either the weight being lifted is increased, the tempo is changed, the recovery period is reduced or a new exercise for the same muscle group is introduced.

With repetition changes throughout the program – for example – from 10 to 12 reps or 8 to 10 reps, this may equate to a 5 or 10% increase in weight added to the exercise. A small increase in weight added may actually decrease the specified amount of reps allocated. This is when you gain a good understanding of your true training repetition range adapted into a strength cycle. Hence, when 12 repetitions of one exercise becomes easy for the 2-3 sets completed, a 5% increase may be added at your next training session. This 5% increase may result in a smaller amount of repetitions being performed, but that's the key because this is when the body really starts to work. The idea is to stay with this weight until this too becomes easy, then increase the weight again in small increments. These ongoing changes never allow the body to adapt and changes in body shape and muscle tone will occur.

Training Progression

Prior to starting any exercise in your program always perform a very light warm-up set of the exercise to prepare you physically and mentally. Beginners should use slow, controlled movements with a continuous flow when starting out – avoid stopping – instead keep the movement flowing until all reps are completed. This keeps the muscle under tension for the whole set and is where real strength gains occur. Over many months of training the speed and power of the movement will increase due to the amount of weight being lifted. As a result, the firing and strength of the nervous system function may also improve resulting in better muscle coordination and an increase in one's metabolic rate that leans up muscle tissue and burns fat more effectively.

A basic beginner's routine (as shown in the previous table) consists of 1 to 3 sets for each major muscle group, with 10 to 15 reps performed per set. Between sets you rest for approximately 60–120 seconds or more, until you feel ready to tackle the exercise again. You'll want longer rests of 120–180 seconds between sets of more complex or higher intensity power exercises in the future. The rest period is also a great time to stretch or complete less strenuous exercises such as training the abdominal region to help maximize training time and drink some water to replenish the body. Another rule of thumb in terms of rest relates to the amount of time before training the same muscle group again. It is recommended that once reps of less than 8-10 are being used, at least 48 hours of rest time is required before training the same muscle groups again. Various research shows that training programs should limit periods of complete inactivity to no more than two to three weeks. Prolonged periods of inactivity should be avoided and the training program should incorporate some form of body maintenance training where a prolonged break is desired.

When you are first starting out and figuring out what weights are good for you, you'll have to go through some trial and error to find the correct weight. It is my recommendation that before you start any exercise or training program that you seek your doctors approval and train under the supervision of a qualified fitness professional to learn the exercises and train with good form. Essentially, lift a lighter weight for between 10 to 15 reps with good form. The 10 to 15 repetition range is based on the principle that beginners should use slightly lower weight for the

THE BODY COACH

first month, in order to allow their connective tissue, muscles and nervous system time to adapt to the loading.

In terms of how fast or slow you should lift a weight is often referred to as the tempo or the speed at which you execute each rep. For example, when performing a bench press exercise, a tempo of '3–3' would refer to the up and down movement time (concentric and eccentric pathway) involved in each repetition – 3-seconds up and 3-seconds down in a continuous flowing motion. The tempo will change from time to time, generally as the weight becomes heavier. A '3-1-3' tempo of the same exercise simply refers to 3-seconds pushing, 1 second holding at the top of the movement and 3-seconds lowering. The tempo of the exercise itself is another way of improving strength using the same weight. In some cases, instead of increasing the weight being lifted when it becomes easier over the weeks ahead, the tempo (time) can be changed to increase the intensity making it more challenging such as a 4-4 tempo.

Now, I know you have a lot to think about already, being a beginner and all, so don't worry too much about counting out the speed of your reps perfectly. Just think slow and controlled for now breathing out when using force and breathing in with recovery. A slow, controlled rep allows you to learn the movement whilst breathing deeply in and out and be sure that you are executing it with good form.

In summary, the training intensity can be modified by changing the number of reps and sets, the weight being lifted, the tempo of the movement, length of rest period between sets and the type of exercise for the muscle group being performed. These elements and many other terms such a split workouts, drop sets, pyramid sets, super sets and many more terms will come into play the more involved in strength training you become. But for now, just stick to the basics so things don't become too complex. This allows you to build a good strength foundation to build upon. The development of all-round strength is best achieved via circuit training using light loads for 10-15 reps and then progressing this 4-week period to specific strength training with higher loads as outlined.

Isolated and Compound Movements

Isolated exercises refer to those that focus on one specific target muscle group, generally involving the use of one joint only. For example, the biceps arm curl exercise (elbow joint) specifically targets the biceps muscle group of the upper arm.

Isolated Exercise – Biceps Curl　　　　　**Compound Exercise – Squat**

Whilst on the other hand, compound movements involve more than one joint such as movement at the ankle, knee, and hip as happens in a squat. In most instances, the larger muscle groups form the basis of one's routine. Common compound movements are squats, presses, pull-ups, push-ups, and rows, as well as the Olympic lifts and their assistance exercises (such as pulls, presses, shrugs on toes, etc.).

Ideally more difficult **compound** movements which use **multiple** joints and muscles are placed first in the workout, while simpler isolated exercises which move only one joint (such as biceps curls or leg extension) are placed towards the end. Usually exercises for torso musculature (abdominals, obliques, lower back) are also placed at the end in order to ensure that they are fresh for more demanding exercises in the beginning, and able to provide as much torso support as possible. Otherwise the abdominal muscles can have their own separate

THE BODY COACH

training routine away from the gym. (see The Body Coach® *Awesome Abs* and *Core Strength* books)

The 3B's Principle™ of Strength Training

Every strength exercise has a number of key elements to consider when setting up and performing a movement. Applying correct technique from the onset will help strengthen the body and the mind. Building strength relies on correct recruitment of the appropriate muscles at all times. The key elements required in order to maintain good body position whilst exercising fall under a classification I've termed the 3B's Principle™:

1	Brace
2	Breath
3	Body Position

1.   Brace

(1a)   Neutral Spine
The term 'neutral spine' refers to the natural alignment of the spine. To help improve the health of our spine, it is important to develop better awareness of our body position by practicing the 'neutral spine' position – sitting, kneeling, lying (front and back), standing and moving. Regular practice in these positions helps develop a sense of control into our muscle memory, so in time we adjust these positions naturally.

A good starting point in finding neutral spine position is by lying on your back with your knees bent (as shown). As you begin to move your spine and pelvis gently through a range of motion by flattening the lower back to the ground then arching upwards – the goal is to find a mid-point between the two that makes you feel comfortable. This is called neutral spine position. A similar movement of the pelvic region is used when sitting and standing.

The main curves of the spine are:

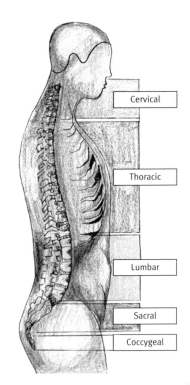

- **Cervical spine (C1-C7):** the rear of the neck curves slightly inwards
- **Thoracic spine (T1-T12):** the upper to mid area of the back curves slightly outwards
- **Lumbar spine (L1-L5):** the lower back curves slightly inwards
- **Sacral spine (S1-S5):** the bottom of your spine curves slightly outwards and links to the coccygeal

Cervical

Thoracic

Lumbar

Sacral

Coccygeal

(1b) Abdominal Bracing

Abdominal bracing is important because it teaches you to contract your stomach muscles, increasing awareness of your body position as well as helping protect your lower back region. The combination of the 3B's Principle™ when training is essential to adapt and master, as it will enhance movement mechanics and maximize training benefits. Abdominal bracing in association with neutral spine position holds an important role in maintaining good posture and can be performed sitting, lying, kneeling, standing or walking throughout the day. Practised regularly you will naturally learn to apply a good postural body position.

In the **4-point kneeling position**, on your hands and knees, as shown below, draw your belly (navel) button inwards towards your spine and hold without changing your neutral spine position. Using deep breaths continue breathing in through your nose and out your mouth whilst holding this inwards braced position of the stomach for five breaths or more. Relax and repeat. Initially, breathing may feel short and the stomach hard to hold in, but with practice you will improve your ability to brace and breathe more efficiently, without tensing other muscles of the body.

Stomach Muscles Relaxed

Stomach Muscle Braced and Neutral Spine Maintained

The goal of the 3B's Principle™ in exercise is to brace the abdominal muscles whilst maintaining neutral spine position and a deep breathing pattern throughout every strength exercise. The 3B's Principle™ helps you get set and maintain focus on the right body position at all times.

2. Breathing

Throughout normal everyday activities, the nervous system usually controls respirations automatically to meet the body's demands without our conscious concern. When we are passive or at rest our demands for oxygen are small and breathing is slow and shallow. When there is an increased demand for oxygen, breathing becomes much deeper and swifter. When you start to exercise or move more rapidly, carbon dioxide from the muscle is pushed into the blood. This triggers a signal in the brain to make you breathe faster and deeper so that you supply more oxygenated blood to your working muscles.

One of the main functions of your respiratory system is to get oxygen from the air outside into the blood, and then expel carbon dioxide waste from the blood out into the atmosphere. Although the basic rhythm of respiration is set and coordinated by the respiratory center (neurologically), the rhythm can be modified in response to the demands of the body. In other words, breathing can be controlled voluntarily to some extent through conscious concern.

To maximize training results, draw in air deeply through the nose and breath out in a slow controlled manner through the mouth – through pursed lips (like blowing out candles) for a count of three. This type of breathing results in the lungs being able to take in more air in a controlled manner. As more oxygen is taken into the bloodstream, the muscle's waste product carbon dioxide is expelled more efficiently, especially as you become fitter.

The breathing focus when performing the core-strength exercises is to control the rhythm of one's oxygen supply by being conscious of one's breathing patterns. This requires an approach of breathing tall like a ballet dancer or standing as a prince or princess does whilst maintaining neutral spine and strong abdominal brace position.

In strength training, breathing generally flows in the following way:
- **Breathe out** when you exert a force
- **Breathe in** with recovery

3. Body Position

One's ability to hold a good body position – *neutral spine, effective abdominal brace and deep breathing pattern* – whilst working the extremities, is crucial in terms of reducing stress on the lower back and maximizing core-strength. By adapting the 3B's Principle™ outlined, you will build a unique internal understanding of your body, its muscles and how they respond to various movements. Adapting the posture of a ballet dancer (for example) in terms of body position is one way to ensure good body position is maintained whilst exercising. The overall focus of each exercise should therefore be on quality of the movement by maintaining a good body position.

As one progresses through the exercises and principles as outlined, they will begin to develop a unique understanding of their body, its movement and muscle control. In all exercises, ensure good head, neck, spine and pelvic alignment is maintained at all times with the rest of the body for the development of good posture.

Women and Joint Hypermobility

Hypermobily refers to joints that can move far further than the average person's movement range due to increased muscle length or ligament laxity.

Women seem to be more susceptible than men in terms of hypermobility of joints including the wrist, elbow, shoulder, hip, knee and ankle joints. Some people are hypermobile throughout all their joints while others have specific joint hypermobility. What this means in real terms is that joints hyperextend beyond what is considered normal postural range. Swimmers are one example group with high levels of hypermobility of joints due to the non-weight bearing training environment they train in over many years.

Problems may arise when little is done and the gravitational forces take over at which point pain sets in. For instance, if a person who is hypermobile through the ankle, knee or hip region goes for a run, they are more likely to experience tenderness or pain in these areas due to the workload on supporting structures in terms of stability. Not everyone with hypermobility will suffer pain or problems. As your Body Coach®, my goal is to simply advise you of the implications of what may occur if these elements are not taken into consideration as part of an overall training program. By undergoing a postural assessment by a qualified health professional such as a physiotherapist can help identify these imbalances and offer you a lifestyle solution such as orthotics for your shoes and joint stability exercises.

Probably the most important element to consider for those with hypermobile joints is that some stretches that have become part of a warm-up routine may need to be replaced with stability drills. This is because stretching a hypermobile joint may overstretch ligaments supporting the joint causing a weakening effect rather than protective. Warm-up activities that bring attention to muscle control include isometric holds and bracing drills. In the meantime, ensure close contact with a health professional for specific joint stability exercises that suit your needs. It is especially important for people with hypermobility to focus closely on correct tracking of the arms and legs in movement to avoid locking out the joints (hyperextension). This also helps keep muscles under tension ensuring appropriate strength and stability is achieved. In some instances, you may have to reduce the range of motion of an exercise to ensure joint stability is developed. Attention to detail of the exercise and body position is of high priority – focusing on quality of movement over quantity.

THE BODY COACH

POOR FORM
Push-up exercise

GOOD FORM –
Push-up exercise

Avoid locking out elbows (hyperextension)

Maintain slightly bent arms and never lock them out in order to maintain muscles under tension

Muscle Training

All muscle training in Strength Training for Women falls into two categories:

1 Isometric Training
2 Isotonic Training

Isometric

In isometric or static contractions the muscle contracts but does not shorten, giving no movement. In most instances one part of the body is held isometrically, such as the abdominal region, whilst the target muscle is exercised isotonically.

Isotonic

In isotonic contractions the muscle contracts and shortens, giving movement. Isotonic exercises generally serve as the foundation for nearly all exercises.

Within the isotonic movement a concentric contraction occurs when a muscle shortens in length and develops tension e.g.

the upward movement of a bar in the bench press exercise. Whereas an eccentric contraction involves the development of tension whilst the muscle is being lengthened, e.g. the downward movement of the bar in the bench press exercise.

FITT Principle

The basic principles of fitness and strength training are summed up in the acronym F.I.T.T

- **F – Frequency** = how often
- **I – Intensity** = how hard
- **T – Time** = how long
- **T – Type** = the type of training
  (strength, muscle endurance, power)

Training Schedule

Beginners should work the whole body at least 3 days per week for approximately 30 minutes, with one rest day between workouts and two on the weekends. For example: strength training Monday, Wednesday and Friday. This is important as your muscles rebuild whilst resting.

As you progress towards **Intermediate** and **Advanced** levels, you want to add more exercises to your routine to increase the overload, but target only specific muscle groups. This is called split training, where you might train the upper body 3 days a week and the lower body 3 days a week, including the abdominal muscles. Spreading your workouts over several days will generally decrease the length of each training session, but in turn makes it possible to train at a higher intensity through more exercises being performed targeting one specific muscle group.

There are a number of training splits that can be developed, including 4, 5 and 6-day routines that rotate between various muscle groups. The **upper body** includes the chest, back, shoulders and arms (biceps and triceps). Whereas, the **lower**

body targets the abdominal muscles, lower back, buttocks and leg muscles. The more advanced you become in your training the more specific training becomes to a point where you may only training one muscle group per day which allows you to train almost every day of the week. The following table provides an example training schedule:

LEVEL	Split	Mon	Tue	Wed	Thu	Fri	Sat	Sun
Beginner								
Whole Body	**None**	Whole Body	Rest	Whole Body	Rest	Whole Body	Rest	Rest
Intermediate								
Each body part 2 days a week	4-Day	Upper Body	Lower Body	Rest	Upper Body	Lower Body	Rest	Rest
Advanced								
Perform one session in morning (am)	Daily split	Upper (am)	Rest	Lower (am)	Rest	Upper (am)	Rest	Lower (am)
and one session in evening (pm) on same day		Upper (pm)		Lower (am)		Upper (pm)		Lower (pm)

Weight Training for Over 50's

Strength training benefits all age groups. You should consult your doctor before starting an exercise program and then allow yourself plenty of time to progress slowly and sensibly with the assistance of a fitness professional. It is important that you be careful and cautious when beginning. You will find that a consistent, well-planned exercise program will make you healthier as you begin to look and feel younger. The weights should be light to start with, with good posture and technique emphasized to build muscle endurance.

Warm- up and Cooldown

Warming up prior to exercise increases blood flow and muscle temperature and reduces muscle stiffness which helps improve speed of contraction of a muscle and reduce the risk of injury. In a gym environment there are three stages of a warm-up. The first stage involves gentle aerobic exercise for 5-10 minutes to warm-up the body. The second phase involves stretching every major muscle group of the body to reduce the risk of injury. In saying this, a hypermobile person will require specific instructions from a physiotherapist to the type of warm-up and exercises and stretches they perform. The third phase incorporates completing one light warm-up set prior to each new strength exercise to ensure good range of motion and muscle activation. This warm-up set does not contribute to the overall sets to be completed.

At the end of a training session, a 5-10 minute cooldown period such as walking or stationary bike is required to decrease body temperature, remove waste products from the working muscles and to increase range of movement. Static stretches are more appropriate to the cooldown as they help muscles to relax and increase their range of movement. A cooldown also helps reduce the chances of dizziness or fainting caused by the pooling of venous blood at the extremities.

Ensure plenty of water is consumed whilst working out – at least 2 glasses or more. Always be prepared directely after training also in order to re-fuel the muscles and energy system with a snack such as small tub of yogurt or piece of fruit as well as consuming a well-balanced meal (protein, carbohydrates, fat) within one hour of finishing strength or exercise training.

Chapter 2

Strength Training Exercises

Getting to Know Your Muscles

Front Side of Body   **Rear Side of Body**

Deltoids Muscle (Shoulder)

Trapezius

Pectoralis Muscle (Chest)

Back Muscles (Rear of body)

Biceps Muscle (Front of upper arm)

Triceps Muscle (Rear side of upper arm)

Abdominal Muscle Region

Front Side of Body   **Rear Side of Body**

Back Muscles
(Latissimus Dorsi)

Triceps Muscle
(Rear side of the upper arm)

Abdominals
(Stomach)

Lower Back

Quadriceps
(Thigh)

Gluteal Region
(Buttocks)

Hip Region

Hamstrings

Anterior
Tibialis (shin)

Calves

Each of the movements of the muscles of the body are described by the following terms:

- Abductor – Moves a limb away from the midline
- Adductor – Moves a limb toward the midline
- Extensor – Increases the angle at a joint (extends a limb)
- Flexor – Decreases the angle at a joint (flexes a limb)
- Pronator – Turns a limb to face downwards
- Supinator – Turns a limb to face upwards
- Rotator – Rotates a limb

Chest and Arm Region

The following exercises target both the chest and arm muscles. The primary muscles used include:

- **Pectoralis (Chest) Region** – Large fan-shaped muscle that covers the front of the upper chest.

- **Triceps** – The rear side of the upper arm.

- **Deltoids** – The deltoid muscle covers the shoulder and consists of three distinct segments. Different movements target the different heads. The anterior or front deltoid allows you to raise your arm to the front. The anterior deltoid is worked with push-ups and front dumbbell raises.

Exercise 1: Bench Press (Using Barbell)

Start Position

Description

- Lie on your back on flat bench.
- Grip bar evenly about 1 1/2 times shoulder width apart.
- Maintaining the natural curve of your lower back, brace your stomach.
- Breathe in as you lower the barbell to the midline of your chest
- Breathe out as you press the barbell to arms length
- Maintain a continuous flowing movement at all times until repetitions completed.

THE BODY COACH

Midpoint

Exercise Tips

- Always train under the guidance of a qualified fitness professional
- Apply 3B's Principle™ - Brace, Breath and Body Position
- Always maintain good posture and body alignment by focusing on the task at hand
- Maintain deep breathing throughout each exercise. Breath in on recovery and breath out when exerting a force.
- Stop exercising if you feel unwell, have pain or have difficulty breathing. Do not start exercising again until you have talked with your doctor.

Exercise 2: Chest Press (Machine)

Start Position

Description

- Sit in chest press machine and adjust handle position.
- Place pin in appropriate weight plate to be lifted
- Keeping the natural curve of your lower back, pull your abdominals in.
- Breathe out as you press the bar to arms length.
- Breathe in as you allow the bar to return to chest.
- Maintain a continuous flowing movement at all times until repetitions completed.
- Keep the bar moving at all times in an even and controlled manner in time with your deep breathing.

Note: Machine adjustments will vary between brands.

THE BODY COACH

Midpoint

Exercise Tips

- Always train under the guidance of a qualified fitness professional.
- Apply 3B's Principle™ - Brace, Breath and Body Position.
- Always maintain good posture and body alignment by focusing on the task at hand.
- Maintain deep breathing throughout each exercise. Breath in on recovery and breath out when exerting a force.
- Stop exercising if you feel unwell, have pain or have difficulty breathing. Do not start exercising again until you have talked with your doctor.

Exercise 3: Dumbbell Bench Press

Start Position

Description

- Lie on your back on flat bench.
- Grip dumbbells evenly and raise into air together above chest midline, palms facing towards knees.
- Maintaining the natural curve of your lower back, brace your stomach.
- Breathe in as you simultaneously separate and lower the dumbbells in an arch motion to the side of the body, keeping in line with your chest.
- Breathe out as you press the dumbbells to arms length back together.
- Maintain a continuous flowing movement at all times until repetitions completed.

THE BODY COACH

Midpoint

Exercise Tips

- Always train under the guidance of a qualified fitness professional.
- Apply 3B's Principle™ - Brace, Breath and Body Position.
- Always maintain good posture and body alignment by focusing on the task at hand.
- Maintain deep breathing throughout each exercise. Breath in on recovery and breath out when exerting a force.
- Stop exercising if you feel unwell, have pain or have difficulty breathing. Do not start exercising again until you have talked with your doctor.

Exercise 4: Dumbbell Flyes

Start Position

Description

- Lie on your back on flat bench.
- Grip dumbbells evenly and raise into air together above chest line, palms facing together.
- Maintaining the natural curve of your lower back, brace your stomach.
- Breathe in as you simultaneously separate and lower the dumbbells to the side keeping the arms slightly bent throughout and in line with your chest.
- Breathe out as you raise the dumbbells back together.
- Maintain a continuous flowing movement at all times until repetitions completed.

THE BODY COACH

Midpoint

Exercise Tips

- Always train under the guidance of a qualified fitness professional.
- Apply 3B's Principle™ - Brace, Breath and Body Position.
- Always maintain good posture and body alignment by focusing on the task at hand.
- Maintain deep breathing throughout each exercise. Breath in on recovery and breath out when exerting a force.
- Stop exercising if you feel unwell, have pain or have difficulty breathing. Do not start exercising again until you have talked with your doctor.

Exercise 5: Incline Dumbbell Chest Press

Start Position

Description

- Lie on your back on incline bench.
- Grip dumbbells evenly and raise vertically into the air together with ends of dumbbells touching.
- Maintaining the natural curve of your lower back, brace your stomach.
- Breathe in as you simultaneously separate and lower the dumbbells to the side keeping the arms slightly bend throughout and in line with your chest.
- Breathe out as you raise the dumbbells upwards back together.
- Maintain a continuous flowing movement at all times until repetitions completed.

THE BODY COACH

Midpoint

Exercise Tips

- Always train under the guidance of a qualified fitness professional.
- Apply 3B's Principle™ - Brace, Breath and Body Position.
- Always maintain good posture and body alignment by focusing on the task at hand.
- Maintain deep breathing throughout each exercise. Breath in on recovery and breath out when exerting a force.
- Stop exercising if you feel unwell, have pain or have difficulty breathing. Do not start exercising again until you have talked with your doctor.

Exercise 6: Incline Dumbbell Chest Fly

Start Position

Description

- Lie on your back on incline bench.
- Grip dumbbells evenly and raise into air together above chest and eye line – palms facing together.
- Maintaining the natural curve of your lower back, brace your stomach.
- Breathe in as you simultaneously separate and lower the dumbbells to the side keeping the arms slightly bend throughout and in line with your chest.
- Breathe out as you raise the dumbbells back together.
- Maintain a continuous flowing movement at all times until repetitions completed.

THE BODY COACH

Midpoint

Exercise Tips

- Always train under the guidance of a qualified fitness professional.
- Apply 3B's Principle™ - Brace, Breath and Body Position.
- Always maintain good posture and body alignment by focusing on the task at hand.
- Maintain deep breathing throughout each exercise. Breath in on recovery and breath out when exerting a force.
- Stop exercising if you feel unwell, have pain or have difficulty breathing. Do not start exercising again until you have talked with your doctor.

Exercise 7: Kneeling Push-ups

Start Position

Description

- Kneel on ground with hands shoulder-width apart and eye-line over finger nails.
- Maintaining the natural curve of your lower back, brace your stomach.
- Breathe in as you lower your chest to the ground.
- Breathe out as you press the body to arms length.
- Maintain a continuous flowing movement at all times until repetitions completed.

THE BODY COACH

Midpoint

Exercise Tips

- Always train under the guidance of a qualified fitness professional.
- Apply 3B's Principle™ - Brace, Breath and Body Position.
- Always maintain good posture and body alignment by focusing on the task at hand.
- Maintain deep breathing throughout each exercise. Breath in on recovery and breath out when exerting a force.
- Stop exercising if you feel unwell, have pain or have difficulty breathing. Do not start exercising again until you have talked with your doctor.

Progression: Push-ups on toes

Back and Arm Region

The following exercises target both the back and arm muscles. Exercises include movement through the shoulder blades, shoulder girdle, elbow and wrist joints. The primary muscles used include:

Latissimus dorsi – Large muscles of the mid-back. When properly trained they give the back a nice V shape, making the waist appear smaller. Exercise examples include pull-ups, chin- and pull downs.

Rhomboids – Muscles in the middle of the upper back between the shoulder blades. They're worked during chin-ups and other moves that bring the shoulder blades together.

Trapezius – Upper portion of the back, sometimes referred to as 'traps.' The upper trapezius is the muscle running from the back of the neck to the shoulder and down the back to form a diamond shape.

Biceps – The front side of the upper arm.

Triceps – The rear side of the upper arm.

Exercise 8: Lat Pull Down

Start Position

Description

- Take an overhand grip on bar overhead, wrists straight.
- Place pin in appropriate weight plate to be lifted.
- Sit with your back straight, chest lifted and head in line with your spine.
- Maintaining the natural curve of your lower back, brace your stomach.
- Breathe out as you pull the bar down towards your chest by leaning slightly backwards.
- Breathe in as you allow the bar to return to an upright position in a controlled manner.
- Keep the overhead bar moving at all times in an even and controlled manner in time with your deep breathing.

THE BODY COACH

Midpoint

Exercise Tips

- Always train under the guidance of a qualified fitness professional.
- Apply 3B's Principle™ - Brace, Breath and Body Position.
- Always maintain good posture and body alignment by focusing on the task at hand.
- Maintain deep breathing throughout each exercise. Breath in on recovery and breath out when exerting a force.
- Stop exercising if you feel unwell, have pain or have difficulty breathing. Do not start exercising again until you have talked with your doctor.

Exercise 9: Single-arm Dumbbell Row

Start Position

Description

- Stand sideways on to a bench and place a dumbbell on the floor within arm's reach.
- Place your left knee and left hand on bench, with your hand directly in-line with your shoulder, and lean forwards with back flat.
- Maintaining the natural curve of your lower back, brace your stomach.
- Take an overhand grip on the dumbbell with right hand and lift it off the floor keeping your arm and back straight.
- Breathe out as you pull the dumbbell up toward your chest – keeping your elbow close to your body .
- Breathe in as you lower the dumbbell to arm's length.
- Maintain a continuous flowing movement at all times until repetitions completed.

Repeat movement with opposite arm.

THE BODY COACH

Midpoint

Exercise Tips

- Always train under the guidance of a qualified fitness professional.
- Apply 3B's Principle™ - Brace, Breath and Body Position.
- Always maintain good posture and body alignment by focusing on the task at hand.
- Maintain deep breathing throughout each exercise. Breath in on recovery and breath out when exerting a force.
- Stop exercising if you feel unwell, have pain or have difficulty breathing. Do not start exercising again until you have talked with your doctor.

Exercise 10: Seated Row

Start Position

Description

- Sit forwards on seated row machine and then adjust height of seat and chest pad to fit appropriately.
- Place pin in appropriate weight plate to be lifted.
- With arms at full length hold onto handles.
- Breathe out as you bend your elbows and pull the handles back by your side.
- Breathe in and return arms towards starting position.
- Maintain a continuous flowing movement at all times up repetitions completed.

Note: Machine adjustments will vary between brands.

THE BODY COACH

Midpoint

Exercise Tips

- Always train under the guidance of a qualified fitness professional.
- Apply 3B's Principle™ - Brace, Breath and Body Position.
- Always maintain good posture and body alignment by focusing on the task at hand.
- Maintain deep breathing throughout each exercise. Breath in on recovery and breath out when exerting a force.
- Stop exercising if you feel unwell, have pain or have difficulty breathing. Do not start exercising again until you have talked with your doctor.

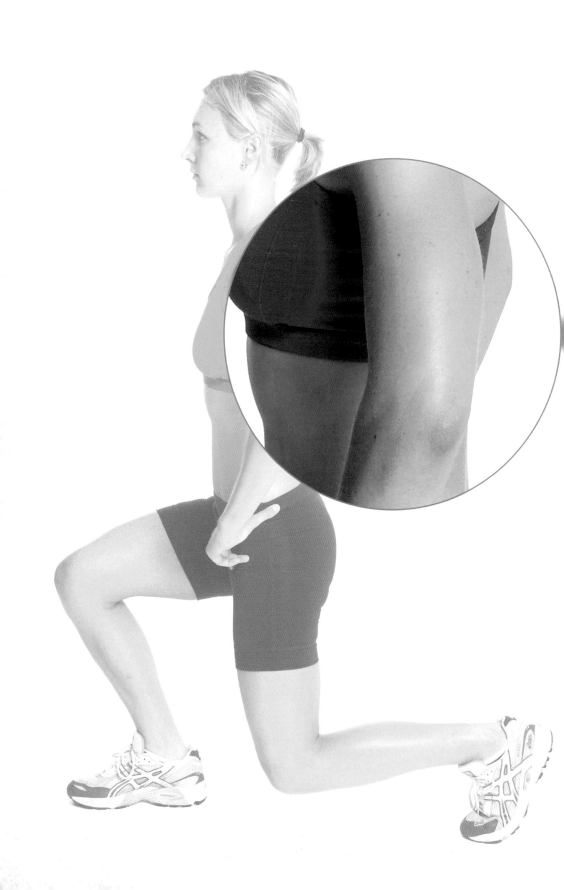

Arm Region

The following exercises target the arm muscles. The primary muscles used include:

Biceps – The front side of the upper arm.

Triceps – The rear side of the upper arm.

Forearm – Bulk of muscle of lower part of arm that leads to wrist and hand

Exercise 11: Barbell Biceps Curl

Start Position

Description

- Stand with your back straight and feet shoulder-width apart, knees slightly bent.
- With your hands shoulder-width apart, take an underhand grip on barbell and rest on the front of your thighs.
- Tuck you upper arms into your body, whilst keeping your wrists straight.
- Maintaining the natural curve of your lower back, brace your stomach.
- Breathe out as you bend your elbows and draw the bar to shoulder height – keeping your elbows close to the body.
- Breathe in as you lower the bars to your thighs.
- Maintain a continuous flowing movement at all times until repetitions completed.

THE BODY COACH

Midpoint

Exercise Tips

- Always train under the guidance of a qualified fitness professional.
- Apply 3B's Principle™ - Brace, Breath and Body Position.
- Always maintain good posture and body alignment by focusing on the task at hand.
- Maintain deep breathing throughout each exercise. Breath in on recovery and breath out when exerting a force.
- Stop exercising if you feel unwell, have pain or have difficulty breathing. Do not start exercising again until you have talked with your doctor.

Exercise 12: Reverse Grip Chin-ups

Start Position

Description

- Take an underhand grip on bar overhead (palms facing towards you), shoulder-width apart.
- Maintaining the natural curve of your lower back, brace your stomach.
- Breathe out as you pull your body upwards leading chin towards bar.
- Breathe in as you lower the body in a controlled manner to the extended starting position.
- Maintain a continuous flowing movement at all times until repetitions completed.

THE BODY COACH

Midpoint

Exercise Tips

- Always train under the guidance of a qualified fitness professional.
- Apply 3B's Principle™ - Brace, Breath and Body Position.
- Always maintain good posture and body alignment by focusing on the task at hand.
- Maintain deep breathing throughout each exercise. Breath in on recovery and breath out when exerting a force.
- Stop exercising if you feel unwell, have pain or have difficulty breathing. Do not start exercising again until you have talked with your doctor.
- For assistance with exercise, place bench under feet and use legs to assist with upper body movement until you become stronger.

Exercise 13: Dumbbell Biceps Curl

Starting Position

Description

- Stand with your back straight and feet shoulder-width apart, knees slightly bent.
- Grip dumbbells and raise to the side of body. Tuck you upper arms into your body, whilst keeping your wrists straight.
- Maintaining the natural curve of your lower back, brace your stomach.
- Breathe out as you bend your elbows and draw the dumbbells simultaneously to shoulder height, twisting the dumbbell as you raise your arm with palms facing towards body.
- Breathe in as you lower the dumbbells to the side of your body.
- Maintain a continuous flowing movement at all times until repetitions completed.
- Variation: Alternate one arm up and down, then the other for a single arm curl.

THE BODY COACH

Midpoint

Exercise Tips

- Always train under the guidance of a qualified fitness professional.
- Apply 3B's Principle™ - Brace, Breath and Body Position.
- Always maintain good posture and body alignment by focusing on the task at hand.
- Maintain deep breathing throughout each exercise. Breath in on recovery and breath out when exerting a force.
- Stop exercising if you feel unwell, have pain or have difficulty breathing. Do not start exercising again until you have talked with your doctor.

Exercise 14: Triceps Pushdown

Starting Position

Description

- Stand with your back straight and feet shoulder-width apart, knees slightly bent.
- Place pin in appropriate weight plate to be lifted.
- Take an overhand grip on the bar, thumbs inwards and close keeping wrists straight (adjust width of grip for added variation in the future).
- Maintaining the natural curve of your lower back, brace your stomach.
- Keep your upper arms and elbows pinned to the body.
- Breathe out as you press the bar down to arm's length.
- Breathe in as you return the bar towards the starting position in a controlled manner.
- Maintain a continuous flowing movement at all times until repetitions completed.

Note: Machine adjustments vary between brands.

THE BODY COACH

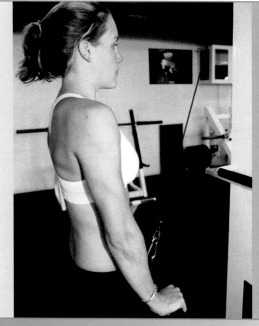

Midpoint

Exercise Tips

- Always train under the guidance of a qualified fitness professional.
- Apply 3B's Principle™ - Brace, Breath and Body Position.
- Always maintain good posture and body alignment by focusing on the task at hand.
- Maintain deep breathing throughout each exercise. Breath in on recovery and breath out when exerting a force.
- Stop exercising if you feel unwell, have pain or have difficulty breathing. Do not start exercising again until you have talked with your doctor.

Exercise 15: Triceps Barbell Press

Starting Position

Description

- Grip barbell shoulder-width apart with an overhand grip (palms facing towards you) and lie on bench.
- Extend arms above chest level.
- Keeping the natural curve of your lower back, pull your abdominals in.
- Breathe in as you slowly lower the bar toward your forehead, bending your elbows and leading with your knuckles.
- Breathe out as you return the barbell to arms length.
- Keep the barbell moving at all times in an even and controlled manner in time with your deep breathing.

THE BODY COACH

Midpoint

Exercise Tips

- Always train under the guidance of a qualified fitness professional.
- Apply 3B's Principle™ - Brace, Breath and Body Position.
- Always maintain good posture and body alignment by focusing on the task at hand.
- Maintain deep breathing throughout each exercise. Breath in on recovery and breath out when exerting a force.
- Stop exercising if you feel unwell, have pain or have difficulty breathing. Do not start exercising again until you have talked with your doctor.

Exercise 16: Triceps Arm Dips

Start Position

Description

- Place hands on edge of bench with legs at 90-degrees.
- Breathe in as you lower your body (buttocks) in a straight line toward the floor until arms at 90-degree angle.
- Ensure arms are kept inwards close to the body and do not splay wide.
- Breathe out as you use the strength of your arms to press upward to the start position.
- Maintain a continuous flowing movement at all times until repetitions completed.

Variation: Raise one leg straight to increase the intensity of the exercise on the arms.

THE BODY COACH

Midpoint

Exercise Tips

- Always train under the guidance of a qualified fitness professional.
- Apply 3B's Principle™ - Brace, Breath and Body Position.
- Always maintain good posture and body alignment by focusing on the task at hand.
- Maintain deep breathing throughout each exercise. Breath in on recovery and breath out when exerting a force.
- Stop exercising if you feel unwell, have pain or have difficulty breathing. Do not start exercising again until you have talked with your doctor.

Shoulder Region

The shoulder joint is a ball and socket joint formed by three bones known as the clavicle, scapula and humerus. The most freely moving joint in the body, the shoulder is dependent on the muscles and ligaments surrounding the joint to stabilize it.

The deltoid muscle covers the shoulder and consists of three distinct segments:

1 **The anterior or front deltoid** allows you to raise your arm to the front.

2 **The medial or middle deltoid** allows you to raise your arm to the side.

3 **The posterior or rear deltoid** allows you to draw your arm backwards when it is perpendicular to the torso.

Different movements target the different heads. The anterior deltoid is worked with push-ups and front dumbbell raises. Standing lateral (side) dumbbell raises target the medial deltoid. Rear dumbbell raises or reverse flies (lying face down on a bench or fitness ball) target the posterior deltoid.

Trapezius – Upper portion of the back, sometimes referred to as 'traps.' The upper trapezius is the muscle running from the back of the neck to the shoulder and down the back to form a diamond shape.

Exercise 17: Dumbbell Shoulder Press

Start Position

Description

- Sit on bench with your back straight, head in line with your spine and feet shoulder-width apart.
- Grip dumbbells and lift to shoulder height, palms facing forward and wrists straight.
- Maintaining the natural curve of your lower back, brace your stomach.
- Breathe out as you press the dumbbells to arm's length overhead and together.
- Breathe in as you lower the dumbbells to shoulder height
- Maintain a continuous flowing movement at all times until repetitions completed.
- Resist any arching of the lower back, by keeping stomach braced.

THE BODY COACH

Midpoint

Exercise Tips

- Always train under the guidance of a qualified fitness professional.
- Apply 3B's Principle™ - Brace, Breath and Body Position.
- Always maintain good posture and body alignment by focusing on the task at hand.
- Maintain deep breathing throughout each exercise. Breath in on recovery and breath out when exerting a force.
- Stop exercising if you feel unwell, have pain or have difficulty breathing. Do not start exercising again until you have talked with your doctor.

Exercise 18: Dumbbell Side Raises

Start Position

Description

- Stand with your back straight and feet shoulder-width apart, knees slightly bent.
- Grip dumbbells and raise to the front of your thighs, arms slightly bent, palms facing together, wrists straight.
- Maintaining the natural curve of your lower back, brace your stomach.
- Breathe out as you extend your arms simultaneously out to the side in a semi-circle, leading with your elbows and knuckles up to shoulder level.
- Breathe in as you lower the dumbbells to the front of your body in a controlled manner.
- Maintain a continuous flowing movement at all times until repetitions completed.

Note: Bend arms slightly to reduce stress and load when beginning.

THE BODY COACH

Midpoint

Exercise Tips

- Always train under the guidance of a qualified fitness professional.
- Apply 3B's Principle™ - Brace, Breath and Body Position.
- Always maintain good posture and body alignment by focusing on the task at hand.
- Maintain deep breathing throughout each exercise. Breath in on recovery and breath out when exerting a force.
- Stop exercising if you feel unwell, have pain or have difficulty breathing. Do not start exercising again until you have talked with your doctor.

Exercise 19: Dumbbell Front Raise

Start Position

Description

- Stand with your back straight and feet shoulder-width apart, knees slightly bent.
- Grip dumbbells and raise to the front of your thighs, arms slightly bent, palms against thigh (knuckles away) and wrists straight.
- Maintaining the natural curve of your lower back, brace your stomach.
- Breathe out as you extend both arms forward until parallel with the ground.
- Breathe in as you lower the dumbbells to the front of your body in a controlled manner.
- Maintain a continuous flowing movement at all times until repetitions completed.

Note: Bend arms slightly to reduce stress and load when beginning.

THE BODY COACH

Midpoint

Exercise Tips

- Always train under the guidance of a qualified fitness professional.
- Apply 3B's Principle™ - Brace, Breath and Body Position.
- Always maintain good posture and body alignment by focusing on the task at hand.
- Maintain deep breathing throughout each exercise. Breath in on recovery and breath out when exerting a force.
- Stop exercising if you feel unwell, have pain or have difficulty breathing. Do not start exercising again until you have talked with your doctor.
- Variation: Single arm raise – Raise one arm, then lower and repeat with opposite arm.

Leg Region

The muscles involved while performing strength exercises for the legs and hip are namely the gluteal region, quadriceps, hamstrings and calves:

Gluteal Region – Often referred to as the buttock region, the primary function is hip extension in unison with the hip stabilizers important in all lower body movements.

Quadriceps – This is the large group of muscles on the front of the upper leg, often referred to as the thighs – starting at the hip joint and ending at the knee joint. Their primary function is to flex the hip and extend the knee, very important in walking, running, jumping, climbing and pedalling a bike.

Hamstrings – This is the group of muscles on the rearside of the upper leg, running from the hip joint to the knee joint. Their primary function is to facilitate flexion of legs, medial and lateral rotation, important for walking, running and jumping.

Calves – The group of muscles further down the back of the leg running from the backside of the knee to the Achilles tendon. They help us to extend our foot at the ankle and flex the toes, which in turn help us in walking, running, pedalling a bike and jumping.

Exercise 20: Leg Press

Starting Position

Description

- Sit in leg press machine and place feet shoulder-width apart on platform.
- Maintaining the natural curve of your lower back, brace your stomach.
- Extend legs and release safety attachment of machine with hands to allow free movement.
- Breathe in lowering your legs at your knees.
- Breathe out as you press and extend the legs away from the body.
- Maintain a continuous flowing movement at all times until repetitions completed.

Note: Machine adjustments will vary between brands.

THE BODY COACH

Midpoint

Exercise Tips

- Always train under the guidance of a qualified fitness professional.
- Apply 3B's Principle™ - Brace, Breath and Body Position.
- Always maintain good posture and body alignment by focusing on the task at hand.
- Maintain deep breathing throughout each exercise. Breath in on recovery and breath out when exerting a force.
- Stop exercising if you feel unwell, have pain or have difficulty breathing. Do not start exercising again until you have talked with your doctor.

Exercise 21: Stationary Lunges – Dumbbells

Starting Position

Description

- Stand with your back straight, one leg forward in lunge position with dumbbells by your side.
- Maintaining the natural curve of your lower back, brace your stomach and raise up onto back toes.
- Breathe in and lower knee towards ground, never touching.
- Breathe out and raise up to starting point.
- Ensure hips are held square at all times.
- Maintain a continuous flowing movement at all times until repetitions completed.
- Complete set and repeat with opposite leg forward.

THE BODY COACH

Midpoint

Exercise Tips

- Always train under the guidance of a qualified fitness professional.
- Apply 3B's Principle™ - Brace, Breath and Body Position.
- Always maintain good posture and body alignment by focusing on the task at hand.
- Maintain deep breathing throughout each exercise. Breath in on recovery and breath out when exerting a force.
- Stop exercising if you feel unwell, have pain or have difficulty breathing. Do not start exercising again until you have talked with your doctor.

Starting Position

Description

- Stand with your back straight, feet together, barbell across back of shoulder.
- Maintaining the natural curve of your lower back, brace your stomach.
- Breathe in and take a lunge step forward with your left foot.
- Check that your feet are facing forward and your right knee is positioned on the midline of your toe and heel. Lower your right knee to 5 cm from the floor.
- Breathe out as you draw your left leg back and stand upright. Push from your heel.
- Repeat action with opposite leg.
- Maintain a continuous flowing movement at all times until repetitions completed.

THE BODY COACH

Midpoint

Exercise Tips

- Always train under the guidance of a qualified fitness professional.
- Apply 3B's Principle™ - Brace, Breath and Body Position.
- Always maintain good posture and body alignment by focusing on the task at hand.
- Maintain deep breathing throughout each exercise. Breath in on recovery and breath out when exerting a force.
- Stop exercising if you feel unwell, have pain or have difficulty breathing. Do not start exercising again until you have talked with your doctor.

Exercise 23: Stationary Barbell Lunges

Starting Position

Description

- Stand with one leg foreward in lunge position with barbell resting across rear of shoulders and upper back.
- Maintaining the natural curve of your lower back, brace your stomach and raise up onto back toes.
- Breathe in and lower rear knee towards ground, never touching.
- Breathe out and raise up to starting position.
- Ensure hips are held square at all times.
- Maintain a continuous flowing movement at all times until repetitions completed.
- Complete set and repeat with opposite leg foreward.

THE BODY COACH

Midpoint

Exercise Tips

- Always train under the guidance of a qualified fitness professional.
- Apply 3B's Principle™ - Brace, Breath and Body Position.
- Always maintain good posture and body alignment by focusing on the task at hand.
- Maintain deep breathing throughout each exercise. Breath in on recovery and breath out when exerting a force.
- Stop exercising if you feel unwell, have pain or have difficulty breathing. Do not start exercising again until you have talked with your doctor.

Start with feet together.
Lunge forward (as shown) and back up to starting position.
(Alternate legs)

THE BODY COACH

Description

- Stand with your back straight, feet together, barbell across back of shoulders.
- Maintaining the natural curve of your lower back, brace your stomach.
- Breathe in and take a lunge step forward with your left foot.
- Check that your feet are facing forward and your right knee is positioned on the midline of your toe and heel.
- Lower your right knee towards the ground, though never touching.
- Breathe out as you draw your left leg back and stand upright. Push from your heel keeping your body tight.
- Repeat lunging forward with opposite leg.
- Maintain a continuous flowing movement at all times until repetitions completed.

Exercise Tips

- Always train under the guidance of a qualified fitness professional.
- Apply 3B's Principle™ - Brace, Breath and Body Position.
- Always maintain good posture and body alignment by focusing on the task at hand.
- Maintain deep breathing throughout each exercise. Breath in on recovery and breath out when exerting a force.
- Stop exercising if you feel unwell, have pain or have difficulty breathing. Do not start exercising again until you have talked with your doctor.

Exercise 25: Calf Raises (Machine)

Starting Position

Description

- Stand on edge of step on balls of feet with heels lowered.
- On machine: place shoulders under pads and straighten body.
- Breathe out as you press up on the balls onto your toes.
- Breathe in as you lower down pointing your heels at the floor.
- Keep the body tight and abdominal muscles braced at all times.
- Maintain a continuous flowing movement at all times until repetitions completed.

Note: Calf raises can be performed with or without an exercise machine.

Note: Machine adjustments will vary between brands.

THE BODY COACH

Midpoint

Exercise Tips

- Always train under the guidance of a qualified fitness professional.
- Apply 3B's Principle™ - Brace, Breath and Body Position.
- Always maintain good posture and body alignment by focusing on the task at hand.
- Maintain deep breathing throughout each exercise. Breath in on recovery and breath out when exerting a force.
- Stop exercising if you feel unwell, have pain or have difficulty breathing. Do not start exercising again until you have talked with your doctor.

Exercise 26: Leg Curl (Hamstrings)

Starting Position

Description

- Lie face down with lower calf and heel region placed under roller pad.
- Place pin in appropriate weight plate to be lifted.
- Maintaining the natural curve of your lower back, brace your stomach.
- Breathe out as you bend your knees and curl your feet toward your buttocks – keeping your hips firmly on the bench.
- Breathe in as you lower your legs towards starting position.
- Avoid the weighted stack touching or body relaxing.
- Maintain a continuous flowing movement at all times until repetitions completed.

THE BODY COACH

Midpoint

Exercise Tips

- Always train under the guidance of a qualified fitness professional.
- Apply 3B's Principle™ - Brace, Breath and Body Position.
- Always maintain good posture and body alignment by focusing on the task at hand.
- Maintain deep breathing throughout each exercise. Breath in on recovery and breath out when exerting a force.
- Stop exercising if you feel unwell, have pain or have difficulty breathing. Do not start exercising again until you have talked with your doctor.

Exercise 27: Leg Extension (Quadriceps)

Starting Position

Description

- Sit in leg extension machine with shin region resting against pads – adjust appropriately – and flex feet by pulling toes up towards shin and hold.
- Place pin in appropriate weight plate to be lifted.
- Adjust back rest so bent leg (back of knee) is resting on edge of seat.
- Maintaining the natural curve of your lower back, brace your stomach.
- Breathe out as you extend the legs forward until straight.
- Breathe in as you lower your legs leading with your heels.
- Avoid the weighted stack touching or body relaxing.
- Maintain a continuous flowing movement at all times until repetitions completed.

THE BODY COACH

Midpoint

Exercise Tips

- Always train under the guidance of a qualified fitness professional.
- Apply 3B's Principle™ - Brace, Breath and Body Position.
- Always maintain good posture and body alignment by focusing on the task at hand.
- Maintain deep breathing throughout each exercise. Breath in on recovery and breath out when exerting a force.
- Stop exercising if you feel unwell, have pain or have difficulty breathing. Do not start exercising again until you have talked with your doctor.

Exercise 28: Dumbbell Squat

Starting Position

Description

- Stand with feet shoulder-width apart holding one dumbbell in both hands with arms extended down in front of the body between your legs.
- Maintaining the natural curve of your lower back, brace your stomach.
- Breathe in as you slowly bend at your knees, sit back and lower dumbbell towards the ground until legs are at a 90-degree angle.
- Breathe out as you raise body upwards using your legs to starting position.
- Maintain a continuous flowing movement at all times until repetitions completed.

Note: Always keep your arms straight and let the legs do the work. Keep your heels on the floor and resist leaning forward from the hips. Maintain ear over shoulder, over hip over ankle – from side position – and knees following the line of the toes.

THE BODY COACH

Midpoint

Exercise Tips

- Always train under the guidance of a qualified fitness professional.
- Apply 3B's Principle™ - Brace, Breath and Body Position.
- Always maintain good posture and body alignment by focusing on the task at hand.
- Maintain deep breathing throughout each exercise. Breath in on recovery and breath out when exerting a force.
- Stop exercising if you feel unwell, have pain or have difficulty breathing. Do not start exercising again until you have talked with your doctor.

Exercise 29: Barbell Squat

Starting Position

Description

- Stand with feet shoulder-width apart and bar resting across rear of shoulders.
- Maintaining the natural curve of your lower back, brace your stomach.
- Breathe in as you slowly bend at your knees, sit back and lower buttocks towards the ground until legs are at a 90-degree angle.
- Breathe out as you raise your body upwards using your legs to starting position.
- Maintain a continuous flowing movement at all times until repetitions completed.

Note: Keep your heels on the floor and resist leaning forward from the hips. Maintain ear over shoulder, over hip over ankle – from side position – and knees following the line of the toes.

THE BODY COACH

Midpoint

Exercise Tips

- Always train under the guidance of a qualified fitness professional.
- Apply 3B's Principle™ - Brace, Breath and Body Position.
- Always maintain good posture and body alignment by focusing on the task at hand.
- Maintain deep breathing throughout each exercise. Breath in on recovery and breath out when exerting a force.
- Stop exercising if you feel unwell, have pain or have difficulty breathing. Do not start exercising again until you have talked with your doctor.
- Variation: Perform exercise using a squat rack, spotter (trainer) or smith machine, especially as weight lifted becomes heavier.

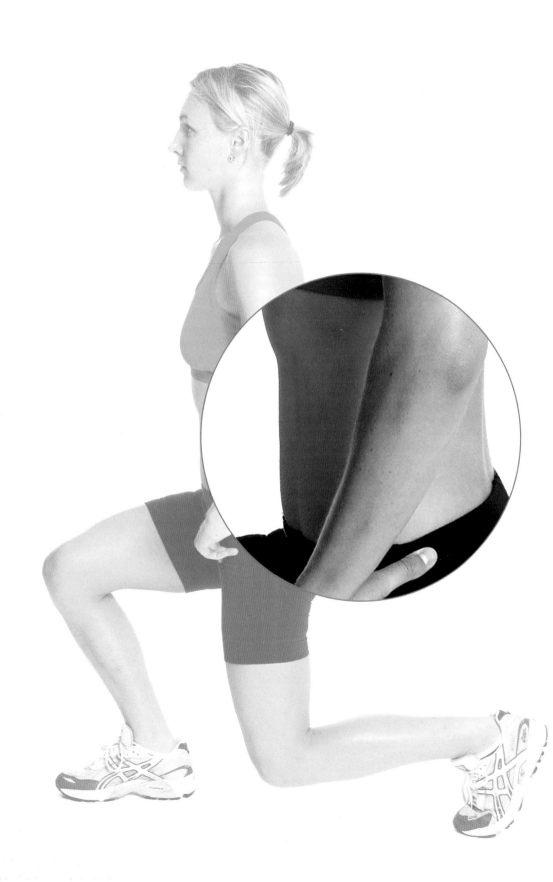

Lower Back and Abdominals

Abdominal wall and lower back musculature requires adequate endurance, strength and coordination for maintaining good posture. The abdominal mechanism consists of 5 major muscle groups:

1 **Rectus abdominis** (six-pack) – Flexion and lateral flexion of trunk

2 **External oblique** – Lateral flexion of the trunk

3 **Internal oblique** – Lateral flexion of the trunk

4 **Transverse abdominus** (deepest muscle layer) – Compresses abdomen

5 **Erector spinae** (back muscle) – Extension of trunk

An exercise for the obliques is found on page 131 – Elbow to Knee. Refer to the Body Coach *Awesome Abs* and *Core Strength* books for additional abdominal (stomach) and lower back exercises.

Exercise 30: Lower Back Extension (Machine)

Starting Position

Description

- Sit in lower back machine with pad across upper back and adjust weight accordingly.
- Maintaining the natural curve of your lower back, brace your stomach.
- Breathe out as you extend the upper body backwards until body is straight (180 degrees). Breathe in as you control the return movement to the starting position.
- Maintain a continuous flowing movement at all times until repetitions completed.

Note: Lower back machines will vary in shape and mechanical design, hence adjust appropriately to suit your body position. If no machine is available use a body weight version of this exercise. Refer to the Body Coach *Awesome Abs* book.

THE BODY COACH

Midpoint

Exercise Tips

- Always train under the guidance of a qualified fitness professional.
- Apply 3B's Principle™ - Brace, Breath and Body Position.
- Always maintain good posture and body alignment by focusing on the task at hand.
- Maintain deep breathing throughout each exercise. Breath in on recovery and breath out when exerting a force.
- Stop exercising if you feel unwell, have pain or have difficulty breathing. Do not start exercising again until you have talked with your doctor.

Exercise 31: Fitness Ball Crunch

Starting Position

Description

- Lie on your back on Fitness Ball with your feet shoulder-width apart, knees bent at 90 degrees and arms resting across chest.
- Breathe out as you lift your shoulders, crunching your chest towards your hips.
- Breathe in as you lower your shoulders back down onto the ball.
- Avoid relaxing stomach muscles. Keep the tension on the stomach at all times until all repetitions are complete.

Note: Rest arms behind head or extend to increase exercise intensity.

THE BODY COACH

Midpoint

Exercise Tips

- Always train under the guidance of a qualified fitness professional.
- Apply 3B's Principle™ - Brace, Breath and Body Position.
- Always maintain good posture and body alignment by focusing on the task at hand.
- Maintain deep breathing throughout each exercise. Breath in on recovery and breath out when exerting a force.
- Stop exercising if you feel unwell, have pain or have difficulty breathing. Do not start exercising again until you have talked with your doctor.

Exercise 32: Abdominal Crunch

Starting Position

Description

- Place LumbAtube™ or half rolled towel under lower back arch.
- Lie on your back with your feet shoulder-width apart, knees bent at 90 degrees, arms extended forward and hands resting on thighs.
- Draw abdominal muscles in and down towards ground and hold.
- Breathe out as you activate your abdominal muscles, lifting your shoulders off the ground, sliding your hands up your thighs towards your knees.
- Breathe in as you lower your back and shoulders to the ground.
- Maintain activation of the stomach at all times until all repetitions are complete.

THE BODY COACH

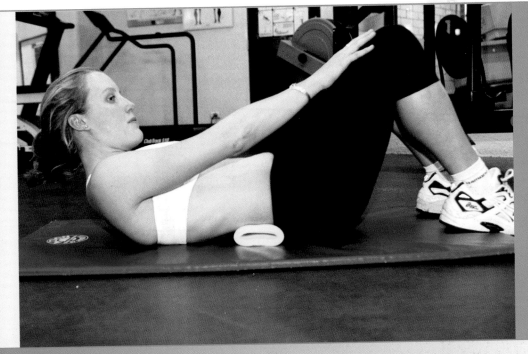

Midpoint

Exercise Tips

- As you become stronger in the abdominal region, remove the lower back support.
- Always train under the guidance of a qualified fitness professional.
- Apply 3B's Principle™ - Brace, Breath and Body Position.
- Always maintain good posture and body alignment by focusing on the task at hand.
- Maintain deep breathing throughout each exercise. Breath in on recovery and breath out when exerting a force.
- Stop exercising if you feel unwell, have pain or have difficulty breathing. Do not start exercising again until you have talked with your doctor.

Exercise 33: Lower Leg Raises

Starting Position

Description

- To target your lower abdominals, lie on your back with your legs vertical in the air and slightly bent with hands beside (or under) your buttocks and rolled towel or LumbAtube™ placed under your neck for support.
- Breathe out as you activate your abdominal muscles (pulling inwards) lifting your lower back and hips off the ground with feet raising towards the ceiling – resist swinging the legs forwards or backwards.
- Breathe in as you lower towards the ground, keeping the tension on the stomach at all times until repetitions are completed.

THE BODY COACH

Midpoint

Exercise Tips

- Always train under the guidance of a qualified fitness professional.
- Apply 3B's Principle™ - Brace, Breath and Body Position.
- Always maintain good posture and body alignment by focusing on the task at hand.
- Maintain deep breathing throughout each exercise. Breath in on recovery and breath out when exerting a force.
- Stop exercising if you feel unwell, have pain or have difficulty breathing. Do not start exercising again until you have talked with your doctor.
- Variation: Lie on bench and hold ends with hands and raise and lower hips.

Chapter 3

Strength Training Routines

Strength training is important for weight loss, raising your metabolism, burning fat, building muscle and keeping your bones and connective tissue strong. It's a good idea to start with machines and utilize the knowledge of a certified fitness professional if you exercise at a gym. Machines are generally easier to use and you'll condition your muscles before moving on to free weights, which requires a bit more coordination and the use of more muscles to stabilize your body.

Getting started

- Warm up with 5-10 minutes of light cardiovascular exercise.
- Perform gentle stretches for the whole body.
- Choose one exercise for each muscle group and do 1 set of 10-15 repetitions of each exercise.
- Rest 60 – 120 seconds between each set.
- Drink at least 2 glasses of water during your workout, then afterwards.
- Start with a program that works all muscle groups and perform 2 or 3 times a week.
- Give yourself at least 24-48 hours to recover before repeating.
- The first few weeks, focus on learning how to do each exercise rather than on how much weight you're lifting.
- After 4 or more weeks of consistent strength training, you can change your routine to make it more demanding.
- Stretch between sets and after your workout.
- Cool down with light cardiovascular exercise and gentle stretching routine.
- Apply strength training cycle to progress development (see graph).

Strength Training Cycles

	Beginner or restarting	General Conditioning	Strength	Power	Maintenance
Sets	1-3	1-3	2-5	2-5	1-2
Reps	10-15	10-12	6-8	3-5	6-10
Percentage (%) of maximum	40-50%	50-60%	60-80%	65-90%	50-80%
Intensity	low	moderate	high	high	moderate
Volume	moderate	moderate/high	moderate	low	moderate

To ensure safe progress with strength training adhere to the following strength training guidelines:

- Gain approval to exercise from your doctor, especially if you are pregnant or have previous injury or heart condition.
- See a physical therapist to assess your posture and joint mechanics and approve appropriate exercises for you.
- Have a physical therapist or certified fitness professional demonstrate each exercise and correct any faults you may have whilst performing them yourself.
- All exercises must be performed under the guidance and supervision of a certified fitness professional or physiotherapist.
- Emphasize quality of movement over quantity.
- Get to know your muscles to understand their function.
- Warm-up the body prior to exercising followed by pre-activity stretching.
- Apply the 3B's Principle™ for helping maintaining correct body posture and maximize your training outcomes.
- Ensure the head and neck maintain neutral position in line with the lower back at all times.
- If at any stage during exercising you feel tension, numbness, dizziness or pain, stop the exercise immediately and seek medical advice.

Beginner Total Body Workout – Once a Week

- Perform exercises in order.
- Beginners set weight to reach muscle fatigue in about 10-15 repetitions.
- Perform only 1 set of each exercise in the first few weeks to allow the muscles, joints and tendons adapt and muscle co-ordination to improve. After which point, increase to 2–3 sets per exercise.
- Rest 60–120 seconds in between each exercise.

1. Chest Press

Sets: 1
Reps: 10-15
Rest: 60-120 seconds

Page: 32

2. Leg Press

Sets: 1
Reps: 10-15
Rest: 60-120 seconds

Page: 76

3. Lat Pull Down

Sets: 1
Reps: 10-15
Rest: 60-120 seconds

Page: 46

4. Barbell Biceps Curl

Sets: 1
Reps: 10-15
Rest: 60-120 seconds

Page: 54

5. Dumbbell Front Raise

Sets: 2-3
Reps: 10-15
Rest: 60-120 seconds

Page: 72

6. Stationary Dumbbell Lunges

Sets: 1 each leg
Reps: 10-15
Rest: 60-120 seconds
Note: Repeat opposite leg

Page: 78

7. Abdominal Crunch

Sets: 1
Reps: 10-15
Rest: 60-120 seconds

Page: 102

Recommendation: All exercises must be performed under the guidance and supervision of a certified fitness professional.

THE BODY COACH

Beginner Split Workout A – Twice a Week

- Perform exercises in order.
- Beginners set weight to reach muscle fatigue in about 10-15 repetitions.
- Perform 2–3 sets of each exercise.
- Rest 60–120 seconds in between each exercise.

Session 1 – Upper Body
1. Bench Press (barbell)

Sets: 2-3
Reps: 10-15
Rest: 60-120 seconds

Page: 30

2. Seated Row

Sets: 2-3
Reps: 10-15
Rest: 60-120 seconds

Page: 50

3. Dumbbell Biceps Curl

Sets: 2-3
Reps: 10-15
Rest: 60-120 seconds

Page: 58

4. Dumbbell Shoulder Press

Sets: 2-3
Reps: 10-15
Rest: 60-120 seconds

Page: 68

Session 2 – Lower Body and Abdominals
1. Leg Press

Sets: 2-3
Reps: 10-15
Rest: 60-120 seconds

Page: 76

2. Leg Curl

Sets: 2-3
Reps: 10-15
Rest: 60-120 seconds

Page: 88

3. Leg Extension

Sets: 2-3
Reps: 10-15
Rest: 60-120 seconds

Page: 90

4. Lower Back Extension Machine

Sets: 2-3
Reps: 10-15
Rest: 60-120 seconds

Page: 98

5. Fitness Ball Abdominal Crunch

Sets: 2-3
Reps: 10-15
Rest: 60-120 seconds

Page: 100

THE BODY COACH

Beginner Split Workout B – Twice a week

- Perform exercises in order.
- Beginners set weight to reach muscle fatigue in about 10-15 repetitions.
- Perform 2–3 sets of each exercise.
- Rest 60–120 seconds in between each exercise.

Session 1 – Upper Body
1. Dumbbell Bench Press

Sets: 2-3
Reps: 10-15
Rest: 60-120 seconds

Page: 34

2. Lat Pull Down

Sets: 2-3
Reps: 10-15
Rest: 60-120 seconds

Page: 46

3. Barbell Biceps Curl

Sets: 2-3
Reps: 10-15
Rest: 60-120 seconds

Page: 54

4. Dumbbell Front Raise

Sets: 2-3
Reps: 10-15
Rest: 60-120 seconds

Page: 72

Session 2(a) – Lower Body
1. Barbell Squat

Sets: 2-3
Reps: 10-15
Rest: 60-120 seconds

Page: 92

2. Stationary Barbell Lunges

Sets: 2 (each leg)
Reps: 10-15
Rest: 60-120 seconds

Page: 82

3. Leg Curl

Sets: 2-3
Reps: 10-15
Rest: 60-120 seconds

Page: 88

4. Calf Raises (Machine)

Sets: 2-3
Reps: 10-15
Rest: 60-120 seconds

Page: 86

THE BODY COACH

Session 2(b) – Abdominals and Lower Back
1. Lower Back Extension Machine

Sets: 2-3
Reps: 10-15
Rest: 60-120 seconds

Page: 98

2. Fitness Ball Abdominal Crunch

Sets: 2-3
Reps: 10-15
Rest: 60-120 seconds

Page: 100

3. Cross-Overs

Sets: 2-3 (each side)
Reps: 10-15
Rest: 60-120 seconds

Page: 131

4. Lower Leg Raises

Sets: 2-3
Reps: 10-15
Rest: 60-120 seconds

Page: 104

Sports Strength Workout – 3 Day Cycle

- Perform exercises in order, 2–3 sets of each exercise.
- Set weight to reach muscle fatigue in about 10-12 repetitions
- Rest 60–120 seconds in between each exercise.
- **Cycle: Week 1:** Upper, Lower, Upper (ie. Monday, Wed, Friday).
  Week 2: Lower, Upper, Lower (ie. Monday, Wed, Friday).

Session 1 – Upper Body
1. Bench Press (Barbell)

Sets: 2-3
Reps: 10-12
Rest: 60-120 seconds

Page: 30

2. Reverse Grip Chin-ups

Sets: 2-3
Reps: 10-12
Rest: 60-120 seconds

Page: 56

3. Dumbbell Shoulder Press

Sets: 2-3
Reps: 10-12
Rest: 60-120 seconds

Page: 68

4. Single arm Dumbbell Row

Sets: 2-3 (each arm)
Reps: 10-12
Rest: 60-120 seconds

Page: 48

THE BODY COACH

Session 2 – Lower Body and Abdominals
1. Barbell Squat

Sets: 2-3
Reps: 10-12
Rest: 60-120 seconds

Page: 94

2. Leg Curl

Sets: 2-3
Reps: 10-12
Rest: 60-120 seconds

Page: 88

3. Alternate Leg Lunges

Sets: 2 (each leg)
Reps: 10-12
Rest: 60-120 seconds

Page: 80

4. Lower Back Extension Machine

Sets: 2-3
Reps: 10-12
Rest: 60-120 seconds

Page: 98

5. Calf Raises (Machine)

Sets: 2-3
Reps: 10-12
Rest: 60-120 seconds

Page: 86

6. Fitness Ball Abdominal Crunch

Sets: 2-3
Reps: 10-15
Rest: 60-120 seconds

Page: 100

7. Kneeling Push-ups

Sets: 2-3
Reps: 10-12
Rest: 60-120 seconds

Page: 42

8. Lower Leg Raises

Sets: 2-3
Reps: 10-15
Rest: 60-120 seconds

Page: 104

Vary abdominal exercises on a regular basis. For more examples, refer to the Body Coach *Awesome Abs* and *Core Strength* books.

THE BODY COACH

Chapter 4

Body
Weight
Workout

Using your own body weight is a great way to strengthen your body if weights are not available. These exercises can be performed anytime, anywhere and its free! In implementing a full body workout you have the option of two approaches: strength training (with rest periods) or circuit training (with little or no rest periods). The key to strength training is to never exercise the same muscle group two days in a row as this allows time for muscles to tone and rebuild. As your strength improves, it's natural that the exercises, reps, sets and routines you perform will need to be modified for improvements to occur. The following workout is designed as a starting point with this process.

Your muscles are the energy burning powerhouse of your body. The better condition they are in, the greater your body's ability is in burning more calories and fat, even whilst you are resting. Strength training itself works in a progressive manner. Initially, we will be working on gaining muscle endurance using light hand weights or performing low intensity body weight exercises over an extended period of time (ie. 30 seconds or more). This approach allows your body, its muscle and joints time to adapt. As you become stronger and more confident, the demand to increase the resistance rises. This is when the body can make changes. In the initial phase of training finding the right exercise to suit your level of strength and ability is important. Undergoing a physical assessment by a qualified health professional such as physiotherapist will help determine the best starting point for you.

Ultimately, the key to effective body changes is when strength exercises start to fatigue muscles at around 8 repetitions (reps) and before 12 (reps). This can be achieved in a number of ways:

• In body weight exercises increasing the lever length, for example, moving from a kneeling push-up to performing push-ups on the hands and toes – increases the demand of the exercise and holding correct body alignment (or posture).

THE BODY COACH

- In strength training, for example lifting free weight (hand weights, dumbbells or barbells) or using weight training machines, it involves increasing the resistance or amount of weight being lifted.

- Alternatively, slowing each repetition of the exercise down to increase the time the muscle is under tension can help make easier exercises become harder. For example, 10 push-ups could easily be performed in 10 seconds if you were fit (ie. 1 second per rep x 10 reps = 10 seconds). Yet, by slowing the exercise down and performing one repetition every 3 seconds increases the time the muscle is being held under tension (ie. 3 seconds per rep x 10 reps = 30 seconds).

- Performing a different exercise that targets the same muscle group. For example, a chin-up exercise using your own body weight and a Lat Pull-down exercise using a weight, target the same muscle group.

Bodyweight Exercise Terminology

Before you get started there are a few key exercise terms you'll need to understand:

- **Repetition** = One execution of an exercise (Rep)

- **Set** = A series of repetitions (ie. 10 reps = 1 set.)

- **Recovery** = Time for muscles to recover after a set before repeating (ie. 30-60 seconds rest)

- **Time under tension** = The speed at which you perform each repetition (ie. 2 seconds lowering, 2 seconds raising)

- **Circuit Training** = A form of muscle endurance training using a light load that works one muscle group (exercise) for a set period (ie. 30 seconds) and then moves onto another exercise with minimal rest in between.

Home and Travel Based Strength Routine

Using your own body weight along with light hand weights is a great way to get started with toning and reshaping your body. These exercises can be performed anytime, anywhere! The key to strength training is to never exercise the same muscle group two days in a row as this allows time for muscles to tone and rebuild. This will depend on how much weight is being lifted as many body weight exercises can be repeated each day – just think of a gymnast in training. As your strength builds, it's natural that the exercises, reps, sets and routines you perform will need to be changed for improvements to occur. The programs below therefore aim to get you started with the process.

Full Body Home Workout

- 2–3 x week - eg. Tuesday and Thursday

Upper Body 1. Routine	Strength Training – Reps, Sets & Recovery	2. Circuit Training – Muscle Endurance
1 Kneeling Push-ups	• 3 sets of 8 – 12 reps.	• Exercise for 15-30 seconds
2 Arm Dips	• Rest 30–60 seconds and then repeat set	• Move directly from one exercise to the next for all 9 exercises
3 Arm Curls	• No rest for exercise that involve per-forming exercise on one side then the other until both sides completed	
4 Half Squat		
5 Stationary Lunge		• Rest one minute at the completion of all 9 exercises and then repeat circuit
6 Single Leg Calf Raises	• If the exercise be-comes easy, slow the tempo down or reduce recovery pe-riods	
7 Stomach Crunch		
8 Cross-Overs		

THE BODY COACH

Before getting started use the following chart to assist in your preparation.

Equipment	• Chair or bench • Hand Weights
Clothing	• Wear comfortable sports clothing
Warm-up	• 3 – 5 minutes of brisk walking to gradually increase heart rate and raise a light sweat to prepare body for the exercises ahead. • Follow this with a period of stretching. Hold stretches for each muscle group for 15-30 seconds.
Workout Time	• 15 minutes (or more) • Exercise to your favorite music • Exercise with a friend
Cool down	• Allow body to return to pre-exercise state with 5-minute cooldown period followed by stretching
Water	• Remember to drink lots of water before, during and after your activity (don't wait until you feel thirsty or start sweating)
Exercise Tips	• Always see your doctor to gain approval to start any new exercise or routine • Brace stomach muscles to support spine • Always maintain good posture and body alignment by focusing on the task at hand • Maintain **deep breathing** throughout each exercise. Breath in on recovery and breath out when exerting a force. • Stop exercising if you feel unwell, have pain or have difficulty breathing. Do not start exercising again until you have talked with your doctor.

1. Kneeling Push-ups (Chest and Arms)

Start   **Midpoint**

Position
Kneel on ground with hands shoulder-width apart. Lean forward so eyeline is forward of fingers. Brace stomach muscles.

Action
Lean forwards as you lower the chest to the ground in line with the hands by bending the elbows, then straighten arms and raise body to starting position. Keep elbows close to the body when lowering and raising.

Option: Perform this exercise standing at an angle with hands on solid table (or kitchen bench).

THE BODY COACH

2. Arm Dips (Triceps)

Start	Midpoint

Position
Place hands on edge of solid chair or bench. Extend legs forward of the body with legs bent at 90 degrees.

Action
Lower body by bending arms towards 90-degree angle. Then, raise body up by straightening arms.

Option: Increase intensity of exercise by extending one leg forward.

3. Arm Curls (Biceps)

Start   **Midpoint**

Position
Standing with feet shoulder-width apart, grip hand weights close to the side of the body with palms facing forwards.

Action
Bend elbows and raise hands to shoulders, then lower and straighten arms.

THE BODY COACH

4. Half-Squat (Legs and Buttocks)

Start   **Midpoint**

Position
Stand with feet shoulder-width apart behind chair. Place hands on chair for support.

Action
Lower body by pushing buttocks backwards and bending at the knees towards 90-degree angle and then raise body up by straightening legs.

Note: When pushing buttocks backwards, ensure feet are always flat on the ground and knees follow alignment of toes (foot angle).

5. Stationary Lunge (Buttocks and Legs)

| Start | Midpoint |

Position
Place hands on hips and extend one leg forward into lunge position.

Action
Lower body by bending both knees simultaneously and lowering rear knee towards floor, then returning to the upright position.

Note: Repeat exercise with opposite leg.

THE BODY COACH

6. Single Leg Calf Raises
   (Balance & Calf Muscles)

Start	Midpoint

Position
Stand tall with hands on hips and one knee raised in front of the body. Brace stomach muscles.

Action
Maintaining good balance, raise up onto toes, then lower. Use chair for balance in initial stages or stand close to a wall for support.

Note: Repeat exercise with opposite leg.

7. Stomach Crunch (Abdominals)

| Start | Midpoint |

Position
Lie on back with knees bent and arms extended forward and resting on thighs.

Action
Raise shoulders off the ground and slide hands up to knees, then lower.

Note: Use a half rolled towel under the lower back to help perform exercise, if necessary.

THE BODY COACH

8. Cross-Overs (Abdominal Obliques)

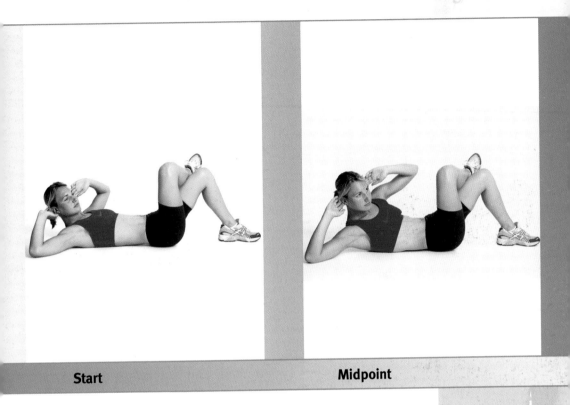

Start   **Midpoint**

Position
Lie on back with knees bent and hands resting behind head. Raise right leg and place foot across opposite thigh.

Action
Raise shoulders and cross left elbow towards right knee, then lower.

Note: Complete set and repeat on opposite side in opposite direction.

Full Body Home Workout Summary

Exercise Summary

Kneeling Push-ups

Arm Dips

Arm Curls

Half Squat

THE BODY COACH

Stationary Lunges

Single Leg Calf Raises

Stomach Crunch

Cross-overs

Chapter 5

Hand Weights – Home and Travel Routine

A set of light hand weights (dumbbells) can be a handy acquisition for women who don't have time to go to a gym or travel extensively. The following hand weight routine is designed to maximize time.

Exercise Tips

- Gain approval to exercise from your doctor, especially if you are pregnant.

- Use light hand weights (dumbbells) only to complete the following exercises.

- Apply the 3B's Principle™ - Brace, Breathe and Body Position for helping maintaining correct body posture and maximize your training outcomes.

- Emphasize quality of movement over quantity.

- Warm-up the body prior to exercising followed by pre-activity stretching.

- Ensure the head and neck maintain neutral position in line with the lower back at all times.

- If at any stage during exercising you feel tension, numbness, dizziness or pain, stop the exercise immediately and seek medical advice.

Strength Format

- Perform exercises separately (ie. Upper or Lower Body) or together.

- Perform continuous circuit style workout for 15–30 seconds – performing one exercise and moving onto the next with minimal rest to build muscle endurance. Repeat circuit 2-3 times.

- General Strength training – perform 10-15 repetitions for 2-3 sets each exercise, resting 60 seconds in-between.

Lower Body Exercises

1. Squat

- Bend arms close to chest
- Squat to 90-degree leg angle then raise

2. Push Press

- Bend arms close to chest
- Squat to 90-degree leg angle then raise arms overhead

3. Stationary Lunges

- Arms by side
- Legs in lunge position
- Lower rear knee to ground then raise
- Repeat other leg

4. Alternate Leg Lunges

- Arms by side, feet together
- Lunge forward then back
- Repeat other leg

THE BODY COACH

Upper Body Exercises

1. Biceps Curl

- Arms extended down, elbows close to body
- Raise arms, then lower

2. Triceps Press

- Extended arms overhead
- Bend elbows and lower weights behind head, then straighten

3. Upright Row

- Arms extended down in front of body
- Raise elbows and hands to chest, then lower

4. Bent Over Row
- Bend slightly forwards, arms extended down
- Brace stomach
- Raise elbows then lower

5. Front Raises

- Arms extended down in front of body
- Raise arms until parallel to ground, then lower

6. Side Raises

- Arms by side
- Raise arms to side until parallel to ground

7. Shoulder Press

- Arms bent, resting weights on chest
- Push hands overhead, then lower

8. 45-Degree Push

- Bend arms and hold at chest height
- Push-out at 45-degree angle, the return

THE BODY COACH

www.thebodycoach.com

International Managing Agent

Saxton Speakers Bureau (Australia)
- Website: www.saxton.com.au
- Email: speakers@saxton.com.au
- Phone: (03) 9811 3500
  International: +61 3 9811 3500

www.thebodycoach.com

Study in Australia

- International Fitness College for overseas students to study sport, fitness and personal training qualifications in Sydney Australia
- 3 month to 2 year student visa courses

www.sportandfitness.com.au

STRENGTH TRAINING FOR WOMEN

Strength Training Index

THE BODY COACH

Photo & Illustration Credits:

Cover Photo: imago sportfotodienst GmbH
Cover Design: Jens Vogelsang
Photos: Mark Donaldson
Illustration p. 18: Svetlana Unger

The Body Coach

Paul Collins
Stretching Basics

ISBN: 978-1-84126-220-8
$ 14.95 US
£ 9.95 UK/€ 14.95

Paul Collins
Fitness Ball Drills

ISBN: 978-1-84126-221-5
$ 14.95 US
£ 9.95 UK/€ 14.95

Paul Collins
Core Strength

ISBN: 978-1-84126-249-9
c. $ 17.95 US
£ 12.95 UK/€ 17.95

Paul Collins
Awesome Abs

ISBN: 978-1-84126-232-1
$ 14.95 US
£ 12.95 UK/€ 14.95

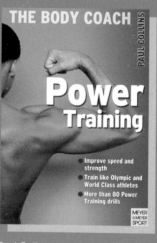

Paul Collins
Power Training

ISBN: 978-1-84126-233-8
$ 14.95 US
£ 9.95 UK/€ 14.95

MEYER
& MEYER
SPORT

www.m-m-sports.com